Silver Burdett Picture Histories

Eighteenth-Century Europe

Pierre Miquel
Illustrated by Pierre Joubert

Translated by Anthea Ridett
from La Vie privée des Hommes: Au temps des guerres en dentelle
first published in France in 1977 by
Librairie Hachette, Paris

© Librairie Hachette, 1977. Adapted and published in the
United States by Silver Burdett Company, Morristown, N.J. 1983 Printing.

ISBN 0-382-06618-9
Library of Congress Catalog Card No. 81-52603

Contents

THE AWAKENING OF EUROPE

As the 18th century dawned, great changes were beginning to sweep through Europe from London to St. Petersburg. Many of them were for the better. To start with, there was a change in the climate; winters became warmer and summers cooler. Harvests were more abundant, and as a result, there were fewer famines. Soon people forgot the hardships of the 17th century.

Everyday life was becoming more comfortable and secure, and the early part of the century was marked by a feeling of optimism. The evils of typhus, the plague, and warfare had not been completely wiped out, but great strides were being made in medicine. In Europe the last great famine was in 1709, and the last great plague in France was in Marseilles in 1720.

This increased security from natural disasters made people more confident about the future and they began to produce larger families. There was an increase in the overall birth rate; within fifty years the total population of Europe grew from 140 million to 175 million. The most numerous were the French, whose population grew to 25 million. In Italy there was an increase from 13 to 17 million, and the Germans managed to make up for the losses of their terrible wars. Russia followed a similar pattern, as did Spain. England began the century with a very small population, about 5 and a half million. This began to increase after 1740 when there was a decline in the death rate, largely owing to improved medicine and midwifery.

This increase in population was of course also linked to a general improvement in the economy. There was a revolution in agricultural methods; land was used more scientifically to produce more and better crops. In northwestern Europe, and above all in England, agricultural techniques improved swiftly and surely. The enclosure of land meant that instead of peasants farming in small, scattered strips, farmers could work large fields and improve the soil by deep plowing and draining. The introduction of fodder crops, like turnips and clover, meant that cattle could be fed through the winter while clover actually nourished the soil so that all the land could be fully used, instead of one third being left to lie fallow every year, as had been done in the past. Agriculture became a science, and gentlemen took pride in becoming farming experts.

In 1700, England was already the most industrialized country in Europe, and the invention of new machines led to many achievements and discoveries. Brilliant inventors opened the way to what was to become the Industrial Revolution. John Kay invented the "flying shuttle" with which weaving could be done at twice the speed. Abraham Darby produced iron smelted with coke. Thomas Newcomen invented a steam engine that could be used in mines and factories. In the Newcastle area, coal was brought out of the mines in wagons which rolled along wooden rails. And in 1750, England was already producing 5 million tons of coal a year. In France and Germany, as in England, commercial groups began to take advantage of the new scientific discoveries to work coal mines in a businesslike way. In France in 1750 the miners of Anzin were digging for coal as deep as 200 meters. It had been discovered that coal was a much better medium for smelting iron than charcoal.

Wherever coal and iron could be found in northwestern Europe, industries began to spring up. And the whole of Europe was becoming rich through the renewal of international trade. Russia and Poland sold timber, wheat, and furs to England, and merchant shipping returned to the Baltic Sea after many years of warfare. The high seas were cleared of pirates by the swift and deadly frigates of the English Royal Navy and the French Royal Marines. Even in the Mediterranean, the Barbary corsairs fled from these royal fleets. The slave market of Algiers was reduced from 30,000 Christians to 3,000. From that time on, Russia was becoming a naval force to be reckoned with. Its entry into commercial shipping was made possible by the opening of the port of St. Petersburg,

The progress of the potato
In 1750 the potato, which had been known since the discovery of the New World, was still grown mainly in gardens. Only in the Low Countries, southern Germany, and Ireland was it cultivated on a wider scale.

The population of Europe in the middle of the 18th century
England and Scotland . . . . 7 million

France . . . . 25 million

Spain . . . . 9 million

Italy . . . . 17 million

Europe as a whole . . . . .175 million

Agriculture in Holland
In 1750 in the Low Countries, 38.6 percent of the cultivated land was devoted to wheat; 24.4 percent to vegetables (beans, peas, and turnips); 15.2 percent to industrial plants (flax and madder); 11.3 percent to oats, 6.1 percent to barley; 2.3 percent to buckweat; and finally, 2.1 percent to potatoes.

founded by Peter the Great at the mouth of the Neva. There were Russian commercial agents in every large European city.

While all this was going on, England and France became the leading countries of Europe. The power of Holland and Portugal was declining; Spain and Italy were in a state of decay. The future of Europe lay in the West with its trade links with the New World. The Atlantic ports rapidly grew rich as they imported the products of the American mines and the tropical produce, like sugar, cocoa, and finally coffee, which had become all the rage with fashionable city dwellers.

While northwestern Europe was being brought to the fore with this influx of new wealth through ventures at sea, in trade, and in industry, economic progress was also taking place in central Europe. Here the monarchs and princes were busy establishing factories, encouraging science and technology, and opening schools and universities. Czar Peter of Russia, King Frederick of Prussia, and Queen Maria Theresa of Austria all decided to westernize their countries and to use their authoritarian powers to achieve an economic growth similar to that which was taking place so successfully in England.

There were major developments, too, in the way people thought about the world. The philosophers of the 18th century were not dry intellectuals concerned only with specialized subjects. They were upholders of liberty and truth, who questioned the injustices of a society in which many people still suffered from poverty and hunger and where freedom was restricted by religion and the class structure. Libertarian thought started in Britain and was spread abroad by French philosophers like Diderot and Voltaire, who were welcomed at the courts of Russia and Prussia. They helped to publish the *Encyclopédia,* illustrated with engravings, which introduced ordinary people to the great technical inventions of the century. It also often attracted the thunderous displeasure of the king of France, with its revolutionary essays on politics, philosophy, and religion.

The manpower of the major
European armies in 1740

France	100,000 men
England	59,000 men
Austria	107,000 men
Russia	230,000 men
Prussia	84,000 men

Encyclopedias

In 1728 the Englishman Ephraim Chambers published his Cyclopedia, *which was translated into French in 1746 by the philosopher Denis Diderot. Diderot became so enthusiastic about the project that he began the production of an enormous reference work in French, the Encyclopédia. His collaborators included the famous mathematician d'Alembert, the abbé de Prades, and Voltaire. There were a number of objections from the Church, particularly the Jesuits. There were also two royal interdictions, but eventually it saw the light of day, and was published between 1751 and 1772—22 years of work! It included 17 volumes of text and 11 volumes of illustrations.*

The Encyclopaedia Britannica *first made its appearance between 1768 and 1771.*

The philosophers' task was not easy. They were in conflict with societies that had scarcely changed since the Middle Ages. Even in the more advanced countries, modern ideas were not accepted without a struggle. In France, the philosophers' writings were burned. The nobility and the Church refused to accept criticisms of a system which made them rich or suggestions that their privileges should be abolished. As to the rulers of eastern and central Europe, while they admired the ideas of Voltaire, the only way they could modernize their armies and industrialize their countries was by continuing their systems of serfdom.

The philosophers fumed when they saw their progressive ideas being put to the service of imperialist systems. The monarchs of eastern Europe were turning warfare into a profitable business, embarking on military campaigns which would increase their incomes, through trade or taxation. The peace treaties they signed took no account of the needs of ordinary people, but were drawn up in the interests of the State. France and England embarked on their colonizing activities from India to Canada and from the Indian Ocean to the Caribbean Sea. Scientific progress was a long way from being reflected in social change. The masses were at the mercy of their ambitious, autocratic rulers.

Nonetheless, in the towns and even in poor country districts, there was at times an atmosphere of gaiety and freedom. In the 18th century, the people of western Europe benefited from improved safeguards against epidemics and famines. They were also better fed, better dressed, and better housed than in the 17th century. Increased wealth brought increased luxury, and the rich middle classes provided entertainment for their friends that tried to imitate the brilliance of the royal courts.

The speed of travel
In the 18th century, sea voyages still took a very long time. To make a round trip from Europe to Brazil would take a year; from Europe to Canton, China, 560 to 650 days; to Peru, 3 or 4 years; and to the Philippines, 5 or 6 years.

Precious metals in the 18th century
Gold
Between 1720 and 1790 the world stock of gold increased by over 100 percent.

Silver
Between 1721 and 1740 and 1781 and 1800, the production of silver increased by 134 percent — from 240,000 to 562,000 kilograms.

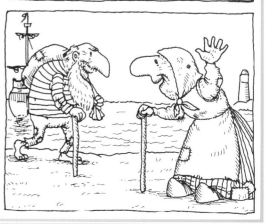

The income of the great European powers in 1740
France ....£200 million
England ....£100 million
Austria ....£80 million
Russia...............£60 million
Prussia ....£30 million

The age of invention

The first industrial machines were invented by practical men who built them to help with their work. In England, John Kay invented the "flying shuttle," which speeded up the weaving process, and Thomas Newcomen built with his own hands a steam engine, which he called a "fire engine." A Frenchman called Villons invented a planing machine in his small workshop, and another Frenchman, Jacques de Vaucanson, later famous for his automatons, designed a slide lathe that made it possible to turn metal cylinders.

In the field of metalworking, most of the new inventions came from Britian. A Worcestershire farmer called Darby set up a smithy on his land for the manufacture of nails and locks. His son, Abraham Darby, taught himself to cast iron pots in sand, and was the first person to smelt iron ore using coke as a fuel rather than charcoal. A Welsh ironmaster, Henry Cort, invented a new metal refining process

called "puddling." A Cumberland farmer, Isaac Wilkinson, made his own iron bellows for his forge, and then invented a steam-powered machine to work the bellows. His son John financed the steam engine designed by the industrialist Matthew Boulton and the Scots engineer James Watt. Watt himself made scientific instruments for Glasgow University. These clever, practical men made a great contribution toward precision engineering.

Fantastic progress was made, too, in optical instrument making, which made possible the great astronomical discoveries of the century. Sir William Herschel, who had a successful career as an organist and music teacher, was an amateur astronomer in his spare time—and the envy of all the professionals! He loved making all kinds of scientific instruments, and built the great telescope through which he was fortunate enough to discover the planet Uranus and its satellites.

In the 18th century, people were interested in doing experiments in physics. They were especially fascinated by the Englishman Sir William Watson's demonstration of static electricity in which a magnetic field was used to attract small pieces of paper.

The Jesuits were not just a religious order, they were scientists, too. In China and Japan, where they went as missionaries in the 17th century, they experimented with measuring distances. They used small but highly accurate telescopes to observe the planets.

In the 18th century, miners started digging coal shafts as deep as 300 meters. However their work was often hampered by underground water. Newcomen, an Englishman, solved the problem by inventing a steam engine for pumping the water out of mines.

Newcomen invented the piston cylinder, which was further developed by James Watt, a maker of scientific instruments. Watt gave it a double action, with two steam jets to work the piston inside the cylinder and a regulator, to keep the engine working at an even pace. Steam-powered machines were built by skilled workmen and were used to work bellows, mills, and looms.

A wave of
new discoveries

European scientists often knew about each other, even if they never met. They wrote to one another, read the special journals that reported the latest discoveries, and published the findings of the groups they belonged to.

The basic sciences had made enormous progress in the previous century, thanks to the work of Sir Isaac Newton, who expounded the laws of gravity, and the German Gottfried Leibniz, who had revolutionized mathematics. At last temperature could be measured, now that the thermometer had been perfected through the work of the Frenchman René Réaumur and the Swede Anders Celsius. The science of measuring heat was the basis of a new technique, the controlled use of steam that enabled machines to transform heat into energy.

But the most fashionable form of physics was electricity, which fascinated everyone. The French abbé Nollet had proved the existence of a mysterious current which up till then was believed to be a liquid. The Leyden jar, a kind of condenser that could store and then release electricity was invented in 1745 in both Holland and Germany. And the American Benjamin Franklin first proved that lightning is an electrical phenomenon.

The Academy of Science in Paris sent out astronomers all over the world to test the theories proposed by Newton in the 17th century; among other findings, they proved that the globe was flattened at the poles.

In England, medicine and the natural sciences took a great leap forward with Edward Jenner's discovery of vaccination against smallpox. And Antoine Lavoisier and Joseph Priestley laid the foundations of modern chemistry. It was not long before their findings were put to use in industry—for in the 18th century, new discoveries were put into practice immediately. Accordingly, measuring the weight of hot air gave an idea to the Montgolfier brothers, paper-manufacturers in France. In June 1783, they launched the Montgolfière, the first hot-air balloon. Soon, people started taking to the air.

The first electric battery was the Leyden jar, invented by scientists to store electricity. Benjamin Franklin used it as a condenser (now called a capacitor) to capture the electrical charge from a bolt of lightning by flying a kite in a violent thunderstorm.

Measuring the position of a ship at sea was difficult, since there were no really accurate instruments. However, optical instrument makers invented the quadrant, and the sextant, which enabled sailors to tell their latitude according to the position of the sun.

In the 18th century one person out of ten died of smallpox, a disfiguring disease transmitted by a virus. The English doctor Edward Jenner saved millions of lives by discovering a vaccination that produced immunization against smallpox.

In 1770 a French engineer, Joseph Cugnot, built the first steam-powered automobile. The machine was fueled by a boiler at the front and couldn't go very far without water. There was no means of stopping it, either—at its trial run it knocked down a wall!

European developments in metal working made it possible to construct bigger and better cannons. From the foundries in Russia came a veritable monster, molded in bronze and richly ornamented, but so enormous that it was unable to fire cannonballs! The Russians still call it the "Czar Cannon." It has been carefully preserved and can be seen today by visitors to the Kremlin Museum in Moscow.

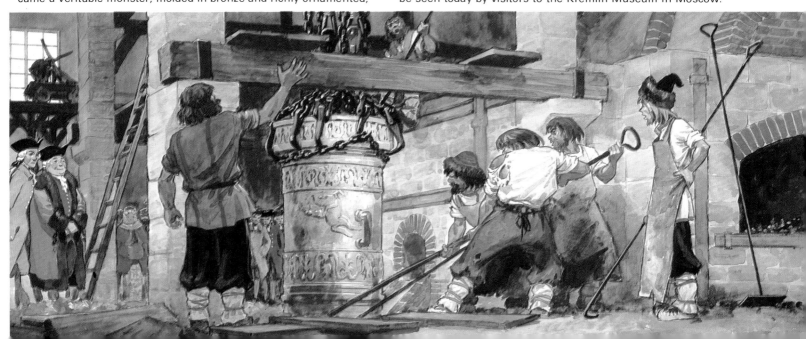

Craftsmen and workers

With the introduction of large factories, the old-fashioned journeyman was on the way out. Mechanization and the large number of workers it involved made it impossible for workers to produce fine individual work or to become masters of their trade. The small workshops began to be replaced by huge, prisonlike factories where goods were mass produced.

Of course, big industrial centers were still the exception. Nevertheless, at Norwich for example, 120,000 people were employed in wool manufacturing, England's largest industry. And in Lyons, the center of the French silk industry, extra labor had to be brought in from country districts, like Savoy and Burgundy. Workers started as apprentices at the age of 15 to 17, sometimes much younger. When they were taken on, their parents had to pay a sum of money to their employer. These apprentices became skilled workers but never real "masters." They handed over the results of their labors to the manufacturers who exploited them and who sometimes grew rich.

In England and France the "captains of industry," the factory owners, hired their workers on a contract basis. Sometimes the employer was also the inventor, merchant, technical expert, and plant manager. He housed his workers and with an eye to the future, got them to put money into a fund for emergencies.

During this process of industrialization, traditional crafts still kept up the old apprenticeship system. Family workshops with one or two apprentices still formed the basis of working life in the cities. But in spite of this adherence to the traditional means of production, the Industrial Revolution was well on its way. The great leap in iron, steel, and coal production was a sure sign of the changes that were on the way.

12

Porcelain, or china, was much appreciated by fashionable people. The best china came from Saxony, from England (manufactured by Wedgwood), and from Sèvres, which produced particularly delicate porcelain. It was also imported from China.

Marquetry is a delicate art in which thin layers of colored wood are glued onto furniture. Rosewood, walnut, pear, and cherry were used to build up designs. The leading English designers were the Adam brothers, Chippendale, Sheraton, and Hepplewhite.

A Frenchman called Réveillon perfected the production of colored wallpaper. The colors were printed by the same methods as were used in textile printing. The rolls of wallpaper were stamped with engraved plates spread with ink.

In Europe the masters of the craftsmen's guilds kept up the religious customs that had been carried down from the Middle Ages. At Lille, France, on May 1, the different trades formed a procession to offer fresh green branches to the patron saints of their guilds.

Gilded wrought iron railings, gates, and doors were very popular in cities and on country estates. Foundry workers formed their molds by hand, rivaling the skill of the blacksmiths, who hammered out their designs on an anvil.

Growth and trade

In the 18th century, city architecture became very beautiful. Much of it can still be admired today, like the Place Stanislas in Nancy, the Nevsky Prospect in St. Petersburg (Leningrad), and the crescents of Bath, which the architect John Wood and his son turned into "the most beautiful city of England." All the capitals of Europe were expanding. In London, St. Paul's cathedral, designed by Sir Christopher Wren, was completed in 1710. The medieval houses on London Bridge were pulled down, and the great Scottish architect Robert Adam designed the Adelphi district between Charing Cross and the Thames. He had a strong influence on a great deal of European architecture.

In England sprawling villages, like Manchester and Liverpool, expanded into towns. While they and London grew outward, cities in France and elsewhere were forced by regulations to grow upward. In Paris the old city walls were pulled down and boulevards, squares, and avenues built. Triumphal arches re-placed the ancient drawbridges, and entire new quarters sprang up. The city became a much healthier place—well-lit, with proper drains and 500 watchmen to keep the peace.

Of course there had to be a lot of money behind all this modernization. Everywhere financial and commercial societies were being formed, especially in coastal areas. France fitted out over 5,000 merchant ships, and she and England overtook Holland and Sweden in naval power. Their trading ships sailed every ocean in the world.

England, France, Holland, and Portugal all took part in the horrible slave trade. From Liverpool, for example, slave ships took Lancashire cotton to Africa to exchange it for slaves. They were taken to America and the West Indies and exchanged again for cargoes of raw cotton, tobacco, and sugar. In 1771, 58 "slavers" sailed from London, 23 from Bristol, and 107 from Liverpool. Some 50,000 slaves were transported by the British that year.

The English and the French created huge sugarcane plantations in the West Indies. The sugarloaves they produced were bought by merchants who sold them at a very high price in Europe. Thus a wealthy class of shipowners began to monopolize the sugar trade.

The Rue Quincampoix in Paris was the French headquarters of the famous East India Company. People rushed to buy shares at £200 and waited until they were worth £20,000 to sell them. When the company collapsed, many of them were ruined.

A wealthy English financier is being carried in a sedan chair to London's stock exchange. Two in the afternoon was the best time to speculate on the exchange. Then, around four o'clock, the business-man would go and dine out in town.

In Germany one of the busiest wool centers was the capital of Silesia, Breslau, annexed by the Prussians in 1742. Frederick II of Prussia encouraged the growth of the textile industry in his kingdom, and Silesian sheep enriched the middle classes of the Breslau region.

In Russia, Peter the Great decided to end the power of the great noblemen. He forced them to shave off their beards, which were a symbol of old Russia, and made them live in St. Petersburg, conforming to the rules of western court etiquette.

Crowded cities

European monarchs were leaving their capitals, finding them noisy, dirty, and unsafe. George III lived at Windsor Castle; Louis XV, at Versailles. The great noblemen of Vienna, Berlin, London, and St. Petersburg owned town houses, but their family home was always in the country.

Cities grew up according to the tastes of the middle classes. The West End of London was made up of beautiful houses built for wealthy merchants. During the same period the "City," the heart of London's business world, was modernized. Between 1763 and 1770, 11,000 houses were built in London's West End. Starting at Westminster Bridge, many of London's streets became wider, cleaner, and well paved.

In Paris, members of parliament and royal officials built themselves splendid houses on the Île de la Cité and in the Marais Quarter. The city planners responsible for the École Militaire and the Place Louis XV (now the famous Place de la Concorde) thought on a grand scale. They had dreams of a city full of wide open spaces and splendid views. But at that time Paris still had 524,000 inhabitants, most of them crowded into unhealthy tenements. When robbery and violence increased, beggars and tramps were arrested wholesale and shut up in hostels called hospitals. At night the streets were lit by 6,000 lanterns. With its wealth of 15 bridges, 25 piers, 18 markets, and 400 hotels, the city attracted a population of travelers, visitors, and students.

London was no better off. For the 500,000 people who lived in the new districts and the suburbs, there were 150,000 crowded into the center of the city. Bundles of straw had to be thrown over the mud of the alleys for George III's coach to pass through. And the traffic was so thick that every day a number of pedestrians were run over. With the smoke from its coal fires adding to the fog, London, despite its street lanterns, was a very gloomy city.

Although the Baltic Sea was shallow, not very salty, and had no strong tides, it was very prosperous. Russian goods were sent from the newly built port of St. Petersburg to arrive at the Baltic ports of Sweden and Denmark. From the Danish port of Wismar, ships left for England loaded with barrels of tar and pine logs, destined for ship building. The Danish fishing fleets also provided fresh fish, which were transported in chests packed with ice to all the ports of the North Sea.

Postal workers sort out mail in a small post office in Paris. The city was already divided into about twenty quarters to which the postmen delivered letters. The envelopes were sealed with wax, but they were not stamped. When they arrived the addressee paid for delivery.

The streets of London were not safe at night. With its tiny alleys and narrow passages, thieves and criminals could easily find hiding places. The only lighting consisted of oil lamps which could hardly be seen in the foggy atmosphere. The lamps were lit with pitch torches.

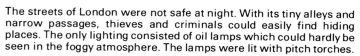

In French towns, lots were drawn among the young men aged sixteen to forty to decide who would serve in the town militia. Soldiers were picked for their height and strength, and grouped into batallions of a hundred men. In wartime they would be part of the regular army.

Europeans loved street entertainers. There were no zoos as yet, and the bear was still a rare animal. Crowds would gather round to watch bear tamers, trained monkeys, and gypsy dancers. This gave pickpockets a splendid opportunity to steal from the bystanders!

Betting, gaming, and coffee drinking

In Europe there were more places opened for the pleasures of smoking, drinking, and taking coffee than for plays or concerts. Coffee houses were a delightful institution. In London and Paris they were meeting places for philosophers, artists, writers, and society women, who liked to go there after the theater or opera. They were the Londoner's second home, and people from the country found them invaluable for catching up with the latest news and ideas.

In Prussia and Austria highly exclusive smoking clubs were formed for the sole use of the aristocracy. Clubs like these followed the British example of being open to members only. Some English clubs were quite wild, like the "Brotherhood of Grey Friars," which had nothing to do with monks. It attracted noblemen like Sir Francis Dashwood, later chancellor of the exchequer, and its meetings were held secretly in caves near West Wycombe. As in most clubs, the members gambled and drank the night away. The painter William Hogarth was a member of the "Sublime Society of Beefeaters" which organized dinners for artists. Its symbol was a grill.

Gambling went on everywhere—in clubs, inns and coffee houses, with money staked on cards, dice, billiards, and bowls. Bets were taken on races, cockfights, boxing matches, and even on the sex of children about to be born to noble families. This English mania became the rage in every big city on the Continent. Paris, too, teemed with gaming clubs and drinking houses.

In Britain, dancing and music were forbidden on Sundays. The working classes went to pleasure gardens or to Bethnal Green for bullbaiting, a cruel sport with none of the pageantry of the Spanish bullfight in Madrid and Seville. There the first permanent stadiums were being built to show off the skills of the most popular matadors, like Pedro Romero and Pepe Hillo.

18

Every coffee house had its own specialty. At Maunoury's in Paris, people played checkers. Will's in London was a meeting place for great literary men—Dryden, Swift, Steele, Addison, and Dr. Johnson. Lloyd's became a center for the selling of wine and ships.

A very fashionable form of entertainment was the magic lantern, which projected pictures painted on glass plates onto a screen. The ancestors of modern filmmakers told the stories out loud as the pictures appeared on the screen one by one.

In England the passion for horseracing took hold. It had been started by James I, who wanted to improve horsebreeding by selecting the finest stallions. Racing started at Epsom in 1782. The English were great gamblers, and racecourse betting became very popular.

The first rhinoceros to be seen by the people of Paris was put on show at the Fair of Saint Germain in 1749. This fair sold everything except books and weapons. Actors and acrobats performed there, calling out to passersby to come and watch their acts.

Frederick William, king of Prussia, was the chief member of the Tabakscollegium, a gathering of aristocratic pipe smokers. The tobacco came from America and Europeans smoked it or took it as snuff. It was rare and expensive, especially in eastern Europe.

Roads, canals, and bridges

The quickest way of getting from town to town was not always by road. Sometimes it was more convenient to go by water. People used boats and barges a great deal on the Thames in England and on the Seine in France. There were regular journeys from Manchester and York to London and from Paris to Rouen. It was a slow method of travel, and going by canal was even slower, averaging 6 kilometers per hour. But the growth of industry speeded up the building of new canals for the shipping of coal and ore. England, with its wealth of natural rivers, was ahead in this field.

The condition of the roads in Europe made traveling difficult, slow, and sometimes dangerous. The post took twenty days to get from Paris to Rome. In Italy the roads were badly maintained and scarcely usable for carriages. The same problem existed in Germany, central Europe, and, of course, Russia, where roads that were passable in summer turned into bogs in fall and spring and into sleigh tracks in winter. It is true that in France, Belgium, and England there were roads that were stone paved or macadamized and regularly repaired. Lined with trees and dotted with posting houses and inns, they were available to travelers, mail coaches, and stagecoaches.

These roads were used by different types of horse-drawn vehicles, from lumbering freight wagons to much swifter carriages. Stagecoaches, drawn by 5 horses, could carry 3 tons of goods and sometimes as many as 30 passengers at a speed of 6 to 10 kilometers an hour, varying according to the condition of the roads.

In France a royal tax was imposed forcing the peasants to contribute towards the building and maintenance of bridges. And Louis XV founded a school especially to train engineers to build roads and bridges. Rivers were still sometimes crossed by ford, but in western Europe stone-built bridges were on the increase. In England there were even bridges made of iron. The first was built in 1779 at Coalbrookdale in Shropshire by the English ironfounder Abraham Darby III.

England, later the first country in Europe to have a railway system, was also the first to set up an extensive network of canals. The horse-drawn barges were used to carry heavy loads. Sometimes an aqueduct bridge was built to take a canal across a river.

When a ship flew the yellow flag no one was allowed to get off or to go on board. It meant she was carrying a serious disease, like smallpox. To avoid spreading infection the crew had to stay aboard for 40 days. *Forty* in French is *quarante*—hence the word *quarantine*.

In France the newly formed department of roads and bridges started a huge program of building royal roads that were well paved and suitable for fast vehicles. In many countries of Europe the roads were mere tracks, and generally unusable in winter. Heavy goods were

There was a postal service in Germany, but not a very good one because of the bad state of the roads. The village postman would take the sealed letters to the mail coach at stopping places set up along the main highways.

almost always carried by river. As far as roads were concerned, France was the most advanced country. The network of royal roads, straight, wide, and bordered with trees, was admired by all the foreign travelers who used them.

Stagecoaches took people from town to town. This picture shows an Italian innkeeper greeting some exhausted travelers from Milan or Venice. The English traveled widely, setting out on the "Grand Tour" of Europe and returning laden with works of art.

Old villages and model farms

Eight English and nine out of ten French lived in the country. Farming was still the main source of national income. In central and eastern Europe, the country villages consisted of tiny, isolated communities hidden in the steppes or in the forest. The people of Europe were still at the mercy of the whims of nature. A season of bad weather and they could be threatened by starvation.

In England, however, agriculture was becoming a science. English gentlemen farmers had learned the usefulness of deep plowing, aerating the soil to make it more fertile, and making full use of rich pasture land. They were already improving the soil with chalk and limestone. They practiced rotation of crops and were growing new grass and root crops which enabled them to feed their cattle through the winter instead of having to slaughter most of them. As a result, animal breeding became much more efficient.

Of course, selective animal breeding could only be done on large estates with money to invest. So the land owning aristocracy moved their tenants out and enclosed their lands, dividing them into separate fields. "Enclosures" took place in France, too, but were limited to a few experiments by big farmers or liberal noblemen.

In France most of the 20 million peasants owned a plot of land, usually small, often less than a hectare. The Church, which owned a fifth of the land, was still employing serfs in some provinces, and the philosopher Voltaire wrote a pamphlet demanding their freedom. But serfdom was not abolished in France until 1779, and it was still practiced a great deal in Prussia. There King Frederick encouraged land clearing and the building of model farms. Vast armies of serfs were required to improve the poor soil of the north, where attempts were made to grow potatoes and rye. They were put under the orders of French and Dutch immigrants whom Frederick had persuaded to come to Prussia to found new villages in return for pastureland, seed, tools, and peasant labor.

In England and France the aristocracy kept a close eye on the care of their horses. They improved their stock by crossbreeding, and racehorses became a source of income. The birth of a foal fathered by a famous winner was a big event on a country estate.

In France, salt was a royal monopoly, and the king kept the price extremely high. Smugglers used to steal it from the mines in Franche-Comté and sell it cheaply. Sometimes they would be chased by excisemen, who would order them to "Halt! In the name of the King!"

English landowners decided to improve their production by enclosing their land so that straying sheep and cattle could no longer trample their crops. The laborers were supervised by surveyors as they placed stakes dipped in pitch to mark out the boundaries of new fields.

The landed gentry were always improving their farming equipment, experimenting with new tools like the sowing plow, which did two tasks at once. George III of England was so interested in these developments that he was known as "Farmer George."

In the 18th century, people everywhere became interested in counting the population. In western Europe this was not too difficult because baptisms were entered on church registers. But in large countries, taking a census was much more difficult. In Russia, officials had to go from village to village to count the local inhabitants. The figures they produced were not very accurate.

The lives of the poor

There was poverty in both east and west. In eastern Europe it was made worse by serfdom. Rural life was still medieval. The aristocracy exacted free labor and money from their peasants, making them pay to bake their bread, grind their corn, and obtain justice. In Prussia during the reign of Frederick II, there was so much misery brought about by war, famine, and disease that the population fell by a fifth. In Poland 20,000 noble families ruled the lives of millions of peasant serfs, and in Russia the situation of the serfs was even worse. Catherine the Great had to send troops to the Volga to put down a rebellion of peasants who dared to demand the abolition of serfdom! Their leader Pougachev claimed to be the late Czar Peter III, who had been assassinated.

Western Europe, on the whole, was a happier place. Life in the country had improved, though abandoned children from the city were shockingly exploited—put to work unpaid on farms, in factories, mines, and mills. In Sweden peasants stopped being serfs in 1750 and became free farmers. In Denmark the peasants were free but had to obey medieval laws. Nowhere, however, was the countryside safe from bands of robbers, often army deserters, who terrorized and stole from the country people, particularly when times were hard.

In the west a new form of poverty appeared in the towns as country folk poured into big cities looking for work. In London and Paris the poor lived in hovels and cellars, in ramshackle warrens full of filth and disease. They found some sort of comfort in gambling and drink, which led to further squalor and violence. People would murder each other to get money to buy gin. Working hours were long—a fourteen-hour day was common—and pay was low. Nor were jobs secure. Employers dismissed their workers at the slightest crisis, so those who were fortunate enough to have work always lived in fear of hunger and poverty.

A soldier returning wounded from the wars could be a useless burden. However, many of them managed to be accepted by finding some sort of work—mending harnesses, shoeing horses, or making hunting weapons. In the evenings they would tell tales about the war.

Townspeople often went hungry. Too many people were coming in from the country looking for work. Churches and charities organized the distribution of free food for the old. Workhouses provided a minimum of food and shelter for the poor in exchange for work.

In England both rich and poor were often burdened by debts. Moneylenders demanded 100% interest! Rich people could offer their family jewels as security. Some lords owed up to £10,000. If they couldn't pay, they were thrown into prison.

"Breaking on the wheel" was a punishment existing in France. The condemned man was tied to a coach wheel set up on an axle and his limbs were broken with an iron bar. Crowds gathered to watch, and the body was left there as a terrible example to them.

When natural disasters occurred, poverty and lack of hygiene made them worse. At Lisbon in 1775, there was a terrible earthquake, claiming 40,000 victims. All Europe heard about it and it inspired the French philosopher Voltaire to write his famous novel, *Candide*.

Epidemics still rage

There were remarkable advances in the theory and practice of medicine and surgery. In 1745 English surgeons were granted a royal charter, and were no longer lumped together with barbers. Also real hospitals were founded. The Edinburgh School of Medicine provided instruction which rivaled that of Leyden, the most famous medical school in Europe. Schools of surgery were started in Vienna and Copenhagen. In France Jean Louis Petit successfully removed gallstones, and Jacques Daviel operated on cataracts by removing the lens of the eye. In 1752 he performed 206 operations all over Europe. In Paris, Friar Come removed kidney stones, while in England, William Cheselden could operate on "the stone" in 54 seconds!

Medicine also made progress. Accurate descriptions were made of heart diseases; the Italians learned how to treat malaria and the English, diabetes. The thermometer became a necessary medical instrument. An Austrian doctor, Leopold Auenbrugger, diagnosed chest diseases by tapping his patients' chests—most of his colleagues thought he was mad! Methods of treatment, however, changed little. Patients were still bled, purged, starved, and given special diets and herbs. As well as arsenic, cinchona, and valerian for the heart, doctors were still ordering remedies like snakeskin and crayfish eyes.

And medicine was not yet able to cope with the terrible epidemics that still raged. Typhus periodically ravaged Europe. In the space of 15 years, whooping cough caused the death of 40,000 Swedish children. Smallpox killed 14,000 Parisians in one year. Imposing quarantines made little difference. In Marseilles in 1720, a plague introduced by ship from Leghorn, Italy, killed 5,000 people. The doctors could do nothing. No one yet knew anything about microbes and viruses.

In the countryside, the surgeon was still often the village barber who did what operations he could, without anesthetics. In France under Louis XV, surgeons were at last given their own Royal Academy, which sent experts out to demonstrate their skills in the provinces.

At the London School of Medicine, students learned newly discovered facts about the human body in anatomy lessons. They could also examine tissues under microscopes and study the anatomical drawings published by special bookshops.

People often took "water cures" at spas in Switzerland, in France, in Germany, and in England. Patients sat in the water and played chess or read books, which they rested on floating planks. The waters were supposed to cure gout, rheumatism, and nervous complaints.

One could get all kinds of remedies at apothecaries' shops. In England they sold "Keyser's Pills," which were supposed to cure scurvy, leprosy, and rheumatism! But they mainly sold potions based on cinchona, medicinal herbs, and spices, such as cloves.

As in the Middle Ages, the townspeople of Europe threw their rubbish into the streets to be cleared away by roadsweepers. In London, King George III had the fashionable squares fenced in so that they were not turned into rubbish dumps overnight.

Growing families

In 1750 the population of western Europe was growing while that of eastern and central Europe was leveling out. Russia had a smaller population than France, and Prussia's was decreasing. But Great Britain was beating all records. In the British Isles there was a fall in the death rate, and people were living longer.

In both town and country, English families had a great many children. The population was growing to such an extent that some people began to worry about it. Towards the end of the century, the economist and churchman Thomas Malthus was predicting that the rising birthrate would bring about the end of the world! English people got married young; the men, at nineteen, and the girls, at fifteen or sixteen. The average family had nine or ten children.

Children added to the workforce in the countryside, and when there were too many, they went to the towns to work in the growing industries. Children did not count for much in family life. On farms they lived like little animals. In towns they roamed the streets. Growing sons were only valued by their fathers so long as they could help support the family. If they couldn't, they were thrown out. Some became soldiers, some laborers, beggars, or thieves. Some left for America. Usually one or two sons stayed behind in the family home. Daughters had no right to family money, which went automatically to the sons and heirs. In wealthy families the girls would receive a dowry, but they were completely subject to their husbands. Young girls could be married off to old men for financial reasons. The eldest son was always his father's heir. The others had to go into the army, the law, or the Church.

In rural Europe, fathers were greatly venerated and their authority respected even when they grew to be very old. In the Caucasus in Russia, a man's hundredth birthday was an occasion to be celebrated in fine style.

Boys of the upper and middle classes were sent away from their families to boarding schools in towns, usually under the jurisdiction of a university. A rich boy might be accompanied by a servant, who would look after him during his school days.

Sometimes the sons of the nobility became colonels at an early age. An eleven-year-old might be given a regiment, paid for by his rich father. He would not lead his men into battle, however. Once he grew up, he would remain at court and just talk about the wars.

When Epiphany was celebrated in Catholic countries, the person who found a bean in his slice of cake became "king" for a day. Well-off townsfolk had Epiphany cakes made with butter, but in poorer country districts people had to make do with buckwheat cakes.

The poor districts of London and Paris were crowded with vagrants and beggars. Parents trained their children to beg outside the doors of churches and restaurants and bring their earnings home at the end of the day. Begging was allowed by the authorities.

In southern Europe there were not many large estates, and the landowning gentry refused to divide them up among their sons. So if they had more than one son, they left their property to the eldest. The second joined the army. In France the king founded military acade-

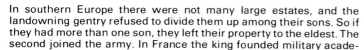

mies for impoverished gentlemen. If a boy was intelligent, he might enter the Church. He would be given a good education at a seminary. The third sons, in England and Europe, usually had to take holy orders, even if they had no real vocation.

Learning and playing

Most of the children of Europe were ignorant. Often they could not read or write. Few went to school, for there were few schools to go to. In Russia those run by the clergy took in only 3,000 pupils in 1725, and half of those were in the Kiev region. The state schools founded by Peter the Great took in only 2,000 pupils over the whole country.

In Protestant countries like Germany, daily Bible reading was the law, and this helped to spread literacy. In Prussia, Frederick II had made education compulsory, but there were not enough schools to go around. Maria Theresa of Austria tried to establish elementary schools.

In England there was a growth of literacy throughout the century. Primary education improved immensely through the charity school movement. Though standards were not very high, it offered schooling to the children of artisans and small shopkeepers.

In France and the Mediterranean countries, education remained in the hands of the clergy. Schools were run by an order of friars, with financial aid from the local parishes. Children went to primary school from the age of six up to eleven or thirteen. Secondary education, available in colleges, was only open to the privileged few. In France the colleges were run by the Jesuits, who had been educating the upper and middle classes for generations. Many of these schools still exist.

In England private schools offered a good education. Latin and Greek were still taught, but so were foreign languages and science. Discipline was always extremely strict.

However, children then, as now, played games. In towns like Birmingham in England and Nuremberg in Bavaria marvelous toys were manufactured for the children of the rich—jointed dolls for girls and splendidly painted lead soldiers which were bought by kings and princes to teach their sons the art of military strategy.

Santa Claus didn't exist in the 18th century, but European children received their gifts on December 6, St. Nicholas's Day. If they didn't behave, they were told that a nasty character called "Papa Birch" would come after them and beat them.

In Russia, grammar schools were started by Peter the Great. Here children were taught to read and write with the aid of printed books. The teachers were priests, and the pupils were usually the privileged children of well-to-do city dwellers.

Most children enjoyed playing with tops—little wooden toys shaped like mushrooms that were kept spinning with a whip. Even very poor children could afford this toy. They would carve their own tops out of pieces of wood, and play with them in the streets.

Children were taught to write with a quill pen made from a goose feather and dipped in ink. The nib had to be cut very carefully so that the children didn't make blots. In village schools, the schoolmaster trimmed them himself. In France, all quill pens were made in Rouen.

The famous Westminster Abbey in London ran a school for wealthy boys, for the rich had to pay for their sons' education. At Westminster, lessons were given by the clergy, and the stress was on reading,

writing, and arithmetic. However, pupils were also taught singing and good manners. The school, which still exists, took in both "day-boys" and boarders. Unruly pupils were frequently beaten.

Philosophy faces censorship

The philosophers of the day had a wide audience, yet rulers often ordered their books burned! In the name of reason, progress, and truth, these scholars and writers questioned monarchical rule, the privileges of the rich, and even established religious beliefs. Very often they fell foul of the royal censorship that defended the established order.

The ideas everyone was talking about started in Britain with George Berkeley, David Hume, and John Locke, who wanted social reform based on the rational, scientific analysis of society. They had a strong influence on the French philosophers, the Baron de Montesquieu, Voltaire, and Jean-Jacques Rousseau. Full of admiration for English freedom of thought, Voltaire once took refuge in England. And Montesquieu made a brief visit there, drawing inspiration from the realistic ideas of the English philosophers.

And if English thought was fashionable in France, the French led the field in the rest of Europe,

for their bold thinking and witty style added force to their arguments. Voltaire, in particular, was outspoken in his denunciations of the vices and injustices of his day. He suffered prison and exile, as did Denis Diderot and Jean d'Alembert, who braved royal disapproval by publishing the *Encyclopédia,* with its revolutionary ideas.

When the State officially opposed the publication of books and pamphlets, they were printed in secret and distributed anonymously.

The ideas of the French philosophers spread as far as St. Petersburg in Russia, where an Academy of Science was founded on the French model. The French language was spoken in the courts, academies, and drawing rooms of all "enlightened" Europe. At the same time, Masonic lodges were multiplying throughout Europe. Frederick II, who supported Voltaire and was fascinated by the new ideas, despite the threat they presented to monarchy, founded the Prussian Grand Lodge in 1738.

In England, France, and Holland, newspapers and journals were published to spread the new ideas. French writers often wrote for the Dutch papers, which were forbidden in Paris because they criticized the established order. However, they were sold there under cover.

"A L'Égide de Minerve" ("Minerva's Shield"). This signboard in French hung over a bookshop in Vienna which sold books printed in France. These books probably included forbidden works like the Encyclopédia in demand by universities and intellectuals.

Printing was still, on the whole, a craft. Here the inking is being done. The type has been set, each letter placed in a kind of frame called a form. The compositor puts them in the case to assemble a page. This is then inked by hand.

In France, seditious books and newspapers were publicly burned, and their writers were liable to be whipped. In England, by contrast, there was a widespread demand for books, pamphlets, and newspapers, which were hardly ever banned.

The Masonic lodge of Prussia was proud of having Frederick II at its head. Freemasonry started in England and spread rapidly through France and then to the whole of Europe and America. Great noblemen and some members of the clergy met secretly in Masonic lodges. English freemasonry upheld belief in God and obedience to the law. The brotherhood's aim was social and religious progress.

The lives of the aristocracy

People "born with silver spoons in their mouths" lived more and more apart from the rest of the world, often at court. The monarchs of Europe had tamed their noblemen, who depended on them for favors, jobs, pensions, and gifts. In Russia the *boyards* paid court at St. Petersburg. The Hungarian nobility had mansions in Vienna. The French lords attended the king's morning arising, called a *levée*. Only princes of the blood were allowed in his chamber while he was still in bed. Very high-ranking nobles were admitted when he got up, and those next in rank were allowed to be present in the king's dressing room. (Some of them spent years intriguing to attain this glory.) To be presented to the king during his stroll was a very special favor. Catherine the Great and Maria Theresa of Austria also surrounded themselves with this kind of elaborate ceremony.

Only in England did the nobility escape court life—they didn't need royal favors. They grew wealthy through their well-run estates or through engaging in trade and industry. The aristocracy left London and built splendid country mansions surrounded by gardens. Landscape gardening moved away from the formal designs of the 17th century, instead creating harmony between buildings and their settings. The famous landscape gardener Capability Brown designed Blenheim Park for the fourth duke of Marlborough, damming a river to create two great lakes. For Lord Hardwicke he designed a group of ponds linked by bridges and a "ruined" castle—the nobility adored ruins and thatched cottages. Plants and trees were imported from the Indies, often very rare species but planted in plenty—as many as 50,000 trees on one estate!

In Paris some private houses were built by foreign lords, like the classical mansion shown in the picture above, now the Palace of the Legion of Honor. It was built for the prince of Salm-Kyrburg on the banks of the Seine. The stone was brought by boat and cut into blocks on the spot.

The English appreciated good food and thoroughly enjoyed elegant or unusual meals. In high society, supper was eaten late, at ten o'clock. People got up late, too. It was considered very fashionable to give an oyster luncheon where the guests devoured dozens of oysters freshly shipped on the Thames River, mostly from Whitstable. When the meal was over, it was the English custom to call for toasts, which would be drunk in French champagne. After that, they drank coffee. The coffee was not as good quality as that drunk on the Continent.

Many women played a part in political life, usually by scheming behind the scenes to help a man to obtain an important government post. Once he was a minister, he could expect to receive visits from grand ladies who took an interest in politics.

Sometimes people at European courts relaxed and played games, enabling the young princesses to mingle with the court clergy. Blind Man's Buff was a favorite. It was a chance to show off the beauty of the ladies and the wit of the men, and it had to be played with style.

This dulcimer player is an automaton, a mechanical doll composed of thousands of moving parts. She is playing a real piece of music. These luxury ''toys'' were developed as a result of the progress in clock-making skills. Court ladies loved such costly objects.

The English court found playing shepherd an amusing pastime. But sheep rearing was also taken very seriously in England, which had specialized in sheep since the Middle Ages. In the 18th century, England led the rest of Europe in animal breeding.

A golden age in the arts

In the 18th century all the arts flourished. The names of musicians, like Handel and Gluck, and painters, like Reynolds, Gainsborough, Fragonard, and Watteau, were spoken with as much respect as the names of generals and princes. All the European capitals wanted the young Mozart to play for them.

There was such enthusiasm for art that people had begun to buy antiques as an investment. Great lords became collectors and archaeologists, and the wealthy English poured into Italy, financing excavations and taking home works of art. Sir Robert Walpole, the first British prime minister, spent £100,000 on his private collection. Fifty peers founded the Dilettanti Society, to help promising artists to travel abroad. "Modern Rome," remarked the political philosopher Montesquieu, "is selling off ancient Rome piece by piece."

Artists who visited the ruins used them in their paintings, and architects and planners longed to build cities along the simple lines of Classicism inspired by ancient Rome. In England this led to houses built in the Palladian style by architects like Lord Burlington. On the Continent, Classicism was overtaken by the Baroque style. With its complex curves it swept through Europe, from the magnificent theater at Versailles to the stucco-decorated churches of Vienna. It even prevailed in the minor arts—miniatures, furniture (the Louis XV style), tableware, and ornaments. The drawing rooms of Europe became filled with a profusion of works of art. Every well-to-do household from Brussels to Milan had to own a Fragonard engraving or a piece of Sèvres porcelain.

In England a great school of landscape painters developed with Richard Wilson, J. R. Cozens, and George Stubbs dominating Europe by the end of the century. And in the world of music, John Gay's *The Beggar's Opera* was performed in 1728: the first ballad opera, in which prose, verse, and music were freely mixed.

36

In 1755 the ruins of Herculaneum and Pompeii began to be excavated. Architects and artists came from all over Europe to make sketches and etchings of the ruined Roman cities, which had been buried by lava when the volcano Vesuvius erupted in A.D. 79.

The custom of taking snuff, which was very fashionable, led to the creation of beautiful snuff boxes. They were made in finely worked gold, and their lids were painted with miniatures showing scenes of court life or mythology. Some of them were true masterpieces.

Mozart, the young musical prodigy from Austria, made a tour of the capitals of Europe while he was still a small child, accompanied by his father. In Rome in 1770, at the age of 14, he wrote down from memory the whole of Allegri's *Miserere* after hearing it played once.

The German composer Christoph Gluck caused an uproar when he had his opera *Iphigenia* sung in French and not, as was the tradition, in Italian. Worse still, he no longer used the harpsichord to accompany the spoken passages. The audience was extremely upset!

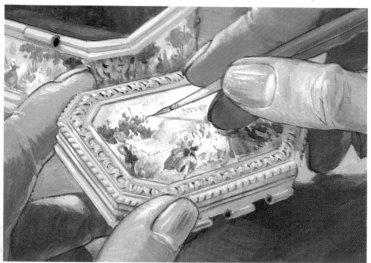

Etchings were engraved on wood or copper with a tool called a burin. The French and Italians were past masters at this art form. Engravings by Fragonard and Tiepolo were printed on paper in this way, in black and white or in color, but always in a limited number.

A world of fashion and elegance

The prosperity enjoyed in western Europe encouraged the birth of new industries. People were full of new, inventive ideas, and in the world of fashion, France led the field.

The royal princesses and marquises who went to fashionable salons took enormous pride in their appearance. They all sought the services of Mademoiselle Bertin, a fashionable dressmaker who visited Queen Marie Antoinette daily at Versailles. She had a shop in Paris from which she sent out dolls wearing miniature versions of her designs to all the wealthy and fashionable Europeans. Orders poured in, including a large number from Russia.

People who could not afford her services tried to copy her models. Printing had made it easier for people to see pictures of the latest fashions. In England, women could read fashion journals which gave detailed descriptions of the Paris collections with their wide-sleeved hooped dresses made of gauze, tulle, and muslin. English ladies had discovered the new, light cotton fabrics imported by the East India Company, originally used as bed hangings. A thriving silk industry grew up in London, too, using skills learned from French refugees.

By contrast, men were dressing more soberly. But if their breeches and high-heeled shoes were not very exciting, they could cut a dash with a wide variety of boots and lacy cravats and cuffs.

Wigmakers became important people. Court ladies, particularly at Versailles, wore elaborate wigs, sometimes enormously high, with models of ships and windmills or stuffed parrots perched on top. There was no limit to their extravagance. One lady wore a model sheepfold full of toy sheep! Men had given up the long hair of the previous century and wore wigs, too, powdered and curled with tongs. The picture below shows a barber's shop where one client is being shaved while another is having his wig powdered, his face protected by a paper mask.

In Paris, London, and Vienna seamstresses worked long hours making silk gowns mounted on hoops, reinforced by bustles and paddings, and decorated with fine, handmade lace. Lace cravats and silken breeches were all the rage among fashion-conscious men.

Three-cornered hats made of felt and fringed with feathers replaced the huge, outrageously decorated hats of the 17th century. They had one drawback—they were very fragile. But a good hatmaker knew how to make them keep their shape, even in the rain.

The hair for wigs was bought cheaply from peasant girls. In England, society women decorated their wigs with fruit, ostrich feathers, and even vegetables. It was not always easy to keep these elaborate structures clean. A rich lady might find a mouse's nest in her wig!

Bootmaking was a highly specialized skill. Boots of the softest leathers from Italy and Spain were individually made to fit. Men's shoes were luxury items, with enormous silver buckles, sometimes decorated with precious stones.

The Spanish mantilla became fashionable throughout Europe. These long silk scarves, embroidered and fringed, were made in Seville. Some were masterpieces of the finest and most delicate work. They enabled women to wear low-cut dresses without getting cold. The mantillas were as popular in the country as they were in the cities, though those sold by peddlers in country districts were made of printed cotton. But young peasant women liked their bright colors and used to wear them to church instead of hats.

Carnivals, water fetes, and masked balls

Feasts and festivals enlivened the whole of Europe. People traveled from all over Europe to attend the Venice Carnival, the "White Night" of St. Petersburg, and the annual Vienna tilting match. In Paris there were over 60 holidays a year. Religious festivals were usually an excuse for enjoyment. On Shrove Tuesday, butcher lads marched through the city to the sound of drums, leading a splendid ox decorated with colored ribbons. In April, a pig fair was held in front of Notre Dame Cathedral, and on May 1 members of the law courts planted a tree, symbol of health and wealth, in the courtyard of the French parliament. Beginning on August 30, Saint Fiacre's Day, there was a nine-day fair in the Place Vendôme, and on Saint Martin's Day in November there was an all-night ball at the Opera.

The festivals of Italy were unparalleled. In Rome the pope's every move was accompanied by pomp. Naples welcomed the arrival of its queen, Marie Caroline, by stopping work and dancing for a week while the fountains ran with wine. On the Piazza Navona every Saturday in summer, there was a water fete when the nobles turned their coaches into gondolas.

England, with no Catholic feasts, was not quite so merry. But every year Bartholomew Fair provided four days of jollity, with exhibitions and sideshows, and May Day was celebrated countrywide with dancing round the beribboned maypole and the crowning of the May queen. Guy Fawkes Day on November 1 was commemorated with bonfires and fireworks. The firework display held in London in 1749 to celebrate the end of the War of the Austrian Succession was so exciting that three spectators were killed! London had its water festivals too. In 1716 the actor Doggett founded a race for Doggett's Badge, rowed by the Thames watermen; it is still held annually. There were pleasure gardens at Vauxhall and Ranelagh. In that brutal age, people also took pleasure from watching executions.

A wedding in the village of Istria (now in Yugoslavia) on the Adriatic coast. The bride is wearing a white dress and a wreath of orange blossom. The men wear leafy twigs in their hats, symbolizing health and wealth. A village lad fires a pistol loaded with blanks. The bride's family has hired musicians to lead the wedding procession with their joyful music. Everyone in those days got married in church. The wedding itself was a solemn occasion, a religious sacrament which united the young couple for the rest of their lives.

The custom of racing riderless Barbary horses through the streets of Rome dated back to ancient times. In 1752 the French duke de Nivernais gave a reception at the Palazzo Farnese in Rome, and he organized a horse race for the townspeople.

The most beautiful Italian festival was the Venice Carnival. The whole town took part, and many foreign visitors, too. Venice was thronged with masked merrymakers who threw confetti at each other and enjoyed trips on the richly decorated gondolas.

Masked balls, which started in Italy, became fashionable all over Europe. Guests often dressed up as Pierrot and Columbine, characters from the Italian commedia dell'arte, or as Turks or Chinese.

On the Seine in Paris, the boatmen used to organize water tournaments on feast days. The public gathered on the river banks or hired windows in houses where they had a good view.

Kings and parliaments face to face

Louis XIV had instituted the rule of absolute monarchy, which soon prevailed all over Europe. In the east, too, rulers wanted to exercise absolute power. The *boyards* who dared oppose Peter the Great of Russia had their heads cut off. Fifty years later, Catherine II held sway over a subdued, tamed aristocracy. In Vienna and Berlin, the "enlightened despots" broke down the opposition of the nobility and took all the power into their own hands. Maria Theresa of Austria governed the Hungarian and Czech aristocracy with an iron hand, typical of her Hapsburg ancestry. In Prussia, Frederick II, known as Frederick the Great, successor to Frederick William, the "Soldier King," ruled alone over a million and a half subjects.

In France under Louis XV, no one seriously questioned the principle of absolute power. It was the foundation of the State. Louis XV could still say, as his great-grandfather had said before him, "I am the State." He had no intention of sharing with his nobles or parliament the authority which he believed was his by divine right. Nevertheless the French parliamentarians continued to oppose the monarchy throughout the century. They wanted to follow the example set by the English Parliament and get the king to respect the laws so that they could have a share in the power.

Two things distinguished Britain from the rest of Europe—the supremacy of Parliament and freedom of speech, press, and person, of which Britons were very proud. The only people to imitate the English constitution were the Swedes. They had a parliament, the Riksdag, the majority of whose members were noblemen. In London the nobles sat in the House of Lords, the House of Commons being filled with wealthy middle-class members. But although the English Parliament controlled the budget, it still had to respect monarchy, whose dominance was accepted throughout Europe. Also, the ordinary people were generally devoted to their kings. Crowds always gathered to see members of royalty passing.

In England the national budget was controlled by members of Parliament, who were elected to sit in the House of Commons for three years. Only wealthier men had the right to vote, and during elections candidates used to bribe people to vote for them.

In the Houses of Parliament in London, the two parties, the Whigs and the Tories, held heated debates every year over the king's budget. So long as they argued instead of voting, no taxes could be levied. Under the English parliamentary system, the king's power was limited.

The highest honor that the French king could bestow was the Order of the Holy Spirit. The Order included only 87 knights and 4 high officers. New members were given a cross of gold and precious stones hung on a wide, sky-blue ribbon.

It was difficult to spread news over the vast Russian empire. When Czarina Catherine II wanted her people to hear news of general interest, she gave instructions to the governors of the provinces to have proclamations from St. Petersburg read out in public.

The French parliament could oppose the king's decisions by refusing to sanction his edicts and orders. But the king had his own method of getting around that—he simply went himself to the meeting of parliament and enforced his own sanctions.

The power of governments

A new kind of administrator was coming into being—the government minister. All over Europe ministers controlled the price of wheat, working regulations, wages, tolls, laws, and taxes. In England the king and the Parliament—made up of the House of Lords and the House of Commons—ruled the country together. The king usually chose his ministers from the House of Lords. These ministers formed the cabinet that governed Britain. In France the 500 king's officers who composed the administration all began their careers in the king's council, where they learned the complex rules of government. The ministers were chosen from among these council members.

In both England and France, the government was led by a prime minister and not directly by the king. It was during the 18th century that the office of prime minister first came into being in England with Sir Robert Walpole, who was in power from 1721 to 1742. He had much more power than the French prime minister, who was dependent on the political intrigues that went on at Versailles; nevertheless the House of Commons could have him removed.

In central and eastern Europe, ministers were very much under the thumb of their authoritarian sovereigns, who changed them whenever they felt like it. Catherine the Great picked cultivated, well-educated Germans for these posts, much to the annoyance of the Russian nobles. The despotic monarchs in eastern Europe used their ministers' services to control everything—justice, the police, internal and external trade, and so on.

In Europe the administration of justice was really in the hands of the State, even though it was claimed in England and France by the members of parliament. They wanted to expound the law and to judge legal complaints—in fact, to take the place of the king. In France this attitude gave rise to a long series of conflicts between the royal administration and parliament.

European law courts still practiced torture as a matter of course—it was called "putting to the question." Accused men were tortured first to obtain the names of their accomplices and again to extract confessions from them before sentence was pronounced.

In England the law was much fairer than elsewhere, though sentences were very harsh. No one could be brought to trial or even arrested unless there was some evidence against him, on the principle that a person is innocent until proved otherwise.

Many convicted criminals, in England and Europe, were branded with a hot iron. The first letter of the name of their crime was burnt into their skin—V for "vagrant," for example. Branding continued in France until the Revolution of 1789.

In Catholic countries the clergy performed many of the jobs that would be done by civil servants today. This Spanish priest is responsible for keeping up the baptismal register. In it he enters the names of newborn children and their parents, and the date of birth.

The Atlantic coast of France was scattered with salt marshes. The right to exploit them was reserved to a royal monopoly called the "Gabelle." The salt had to be weighed by the workers in front of a royal official. At Nantes this was done several times a year. The salt was kept in storage by the Gabelle officials, and later sold to the public. In most regions buyers had to pay very heavy duties on salt.

Merchant shipping and ships of war

The king's sailors were kept busy. In the 18th century, the English Royal Navy and the French Royal Marines were sailing all the oceans of the world. The English were no longer content with simply attacking the king of Spain's galleons. They kept order at sea to ensure the protection of their merchant shipping. The day of the admirals had dawned.

The fleets of the previous century were scuttled. The French fleet in the Levant disbanded its galleys. The last to use galley ships were the Moslems and in the Baltic, the Russians. Admirals commanded ships of the line, frigates, and corvettes with two or three decks able to carry many cannons. Firepower was all-important.

The English Royal Navy owned 8,400 cannons; the French Royal Marines, 5,600. In sea battles each side tried to wipe the other out. On the high seas the squadrons lined up in parallel rows and fired until they ran out of ammunition. Ships' hulls began to be lined with protective copper plates and powerful, hard-hitting cannons were fixed on board.

The role of these great fleets was changing. Their task was to defend merchant shipping rather than to attack enemies. Cruisers accompanied merchant convoys to keep off pirates. Privateering still went on in some seas. Barbary ships still swarmed on the Mediterranean in the service of the Turks. Soon the corvettes of the French buccaneer Surcouf were to decimate English merchant ships and avenge French losses on the coasts of India.

Britain was conscious of her seafaring traditions and proud of a long succession of naval victories. Regular fleets from England and France controlled more and more of the oceans, at the expense of the Dutch and Spanish. A Channel fleet was always in being, and British squadrons kept watch in the Mediterranean and the Caribbean. And of course, the sailors of England and Spain had not yet finished fighting with each other.

Despite competition from the British, the Dutch remained masters of the art of shipbuilding. The "axe masters," the shipbuilders of old, were replaced by marine engineers, who used mathematical calculations to draw up their plans.

Dupleix arriving at the Indian port of Chandernagor. He was one of Louis XV's administrators, and became governor general of French India in 1742. He took it upon himself to throw the British out of India but was defeated by Robert Clive of the East India Company at Arcot.

Turkish and Barbary pirates remained a threat in the Mediterranean. The Turks would make surprise attacks on merchant ships, boarding them and taking Christians prisoner. They kept them in the horrible prisons of Algiers before selling them as slaves.

The last French galleys were dismantled in 1748. Up until then, these great rowing boats had been used by the Royal Mediterranean Fleet, the labor being supplied by brigands and murderers condemned to

penal servitude. On their return to Marseilles their guards allowed them to sell the handiwork they had made on board. Galleys were slow and heavy, and were replaced by swift frigates and sloops.

Officers and gentlemen

In England, France, and elsewhere in Europe, military status was considered an honor. It could also provide an excellent income. Commissions could be bought and sold for each successive army grade. A commission in a cavalry regiment could cost £120,000; an infantry company commission might cost £15,000. Therefore the positions of captain and colonel were reserved for the wealthy. Because of this, many leisured gentlemen with no military experience or indeed any intention of engaging in active service bought commissions. Some troops were led, at least on paper, by twelve-year-old boys! Officers had to recruit their own men, provide them with clothing and lodgings, and train them for warfare. This was no job for twelve-year-olds or inexperienced gentlemen in ruffles and lace.

Fortunately for the French army—which had no fewer than 1,000 generals and 900 colonels—it was not actually led by such inappropriate officers. The real authority was in the hands of lieutenant colonels, hardened in the saddle, poor noblemen who

had trained in the new military academies.

The English army was corrupt, inefficient and unpopular. With no organized police force in England, it was the soldiers who were called out to suppress riots and even strikes. As in France, Austria, and Prussia these men were professionals, but they were poorly paid and army life was brutal. In Britain and Prussia discipline was extremely harsh. Sometimes wrongdoers were flogged to death.

The Prussian army was the best in Europe, with its revolutionary methods of drilling and tactics. The heroic cavalry charges and massed pikemen of the past were replaced by the method of moving from line to column and vice versa. Regiments divided into three columns, one to fire while the second was loading, and the third to have bayonets at the ready against the enemy's horse. The soldiers had to be able to move quickly to change the battle order and avoid losses. Warfare was becoming a science which was taught in schools before being put into practice.

European regiments had had their own uniforms and flags for a long time. The uniform of the French queen's regiment was renewed every three years. Military services lasted for eight years. A young man had to be sixteen to join the army.

In Frederick II's Prussian army, punishments were very harsh. To maneuver the units in a battle, rigorous discipline was essential. Deserters were shot, and men who disobeyed regulations, however minor, had to go through the punishment of "running the gauntlet."

Many soldiers in the French army were mercenaries from Switzerland, Germany, Belgium, Italy, and Scotland. A Scottish sergeant returning home after ten years' campaigning might not have made his fortune, but he would bring back enough to buy himself a farm.

The Prussian army recruiters combed Germany for tall, strong lads to become the king's grenadiers. Recruiting methods were the same everywhere. The officers would get a likely young man drunk so that he signed his enlistment papers in return for a modest sum.

In the wars with the Turks, the Polish cavalry were the fiercest fighters in Europe. Periodically, the green flag of the Turkish sultan led attacks on the towns of central Europe. The Turks were trying to

move into Europe, threatening Vienna, and the Balkans. The Polish noblemen had learned to dread them. Helmeted and armored, the Polish soldiers would charge furiously against the Turkish infantry.

Churches and dissenters

All over Europe the churches were controlled by the State. Peter the Great had seized the fortunes of the clergy and suppressed the patriarch of all the Russias, replacing him with a Holy Synod whose members he chose himself. In Prussia and Austria the despotic rulers dominated the clergy. In France, Italy, Spain, and Portugal, the Jesuits, the "soldiers of the pope," had been expelled. Kings wanted to be the only rulers, even over men's souls.

But the ordinary people were rebelling. Although few were able to read the works of the philosophers who were attacking religion, dissidents were reacting against a faith imposed by kings.

The Church of England was being undermined by the evangelical movement. Methodists, inspired by John Wesley, removed themselves from the official church. Theirs was a religion for the poor, preaching thrift, abstinence, and hard work that aimed to revive Christian belief throughout Britain. The Quakers, members of a Christian sect founded in the previous century, also rejected the established church. They were known for their hard work, interest in social reform, and success in business.

In northern Europe there were dissenters, too. In Germany and Sweden the Pietists were demanding a return to individual faith and the teachings of the Bible. They didn't want a state-run church. Never had faith been so strong among minority groups.

In France the Catholic Church itself was in disarray. Bishops were reading Voltaire, attending anticlerical Masonic meetings, and rejecting the authority of the pope. Louis XVI remarked that it would be a good thing if the archbishop of Paris believed in God! Jansenists were agitating, and Protestants were revolting against the hardening attitude against them of the Catholic Church. Protestant children were being taken from their parents, and girls were forced to enter convents. Protestant marriages were not recognized, and galley slaves included prisoners of conscience. Religious war threatened.

In Belgium it was very important to know the catechism. In country districts the clergy often taught reading, writing, and the catechism at the same time, and children had classes only on a Sunday morning! At church everyone paid great attention to the sermon.

In 1727 in Paris there was a series of miracles at the tomb of a deacon, François Pâris. Everyone rushed there to be healed—the blind, the crippled, the deaf, the dumb. There were so many incidents of mass hysteria that the king ordered the cemetery to be closed.

In England the Quakers were known for their sober dress and behavior and their liking for hard work. They met for worship in meeting houses. Quakers were excluded from holding public office, but they played an important part in industry and banking.

In Protestant Sweden, royal funerals were organized with a great deal of pomp and ceremony. When King Adolf Frederick died in 1771, his son Gustav III, who wanted to restore the power of the monarchy, gave him a magnificent send-off.

In England the Catholics didn't give up their struggle for equality, and in 1778 the Catholic Relief Act gave them more freedom. Priests were no longer imprisoned for saying Mass, and the children of Catholics were allowed to inherit property. However, two years later a Protestant extremist, Lord George Gordon, incited people to plunder Catholic houses, sparking off a six-day riot in London.

The survival of superstition

Ordinary people of the 18th century believed in miracles just as they believed in God. They also believed what they were told by quacks and charlatans. They had a strong belief in the devil, and suspected witches were still persecuted.

Of course, attitudes in western Europe were changing, but country people remained much the same. In England and France, villages were often cut off from the outside world, except for visiting soldiers, pilgrims, and above all peddlers who sold religious pamphlets, almanacs, and fairy tales. Villagers often gathered in the evenings to exchange stories of ghosts and fairies.

In cities, by contrast, the ordinary folk were influenced by their contacts with the upper classes. Information was circulated in newspapers, on posters, in barber shops, and in coffee houses. The working classes of Paris, London, Madrid, and Amsterdam imitated the lives of the nobility.

Dances, songs, and fashions were passed down from one social group to the next. And happiness and freedom were uppermost in everyone's mind.

Despite the general air of festivity in the big cities, the sight of the rich enjoying themselves was painful to those who had nothing to eat. Londoners of the depressed classes could quickly turn to violence, as happened when the Gin Act was passed to check the sale of spirits. The delightful pleasure gardens of Vauxhall and Ranelagh became undisciplined, licentious places. In France there were similar stirrings. Processions and carnivals were forbidden when festivals became occasions for sedition.

Yet the new thinking did not do away with ancient terrors. When an extra large wolf devoured some peasants' sheep in France, it was immediately thought to be the devil. The army had to be brought in to kill it and parade its body from village to village to quiet people's superstitious fears.

52

Europe teemed with highly successful charlatans who sold "magical" potions and powders. Two pinches in a lady's drink, for instance, and she was supposed to fall instantly in love! Charlatans advertised themselves by singing, reciting verses, and playing drums and horns.

The French royal lottery was founded in 1660. In the 18th century, there were lotteries in every European country, even inside the Vatican! A wheel containing numbers was spun, and the winners were drawn by a child with his eyes blindfolded.

Despite progress in science there was still much interest in alchemy, the magical branch of chemistry. In England, people still believed in the existence of the philosopher's stone that could turn other metals into gold. Even the wise Dr. Johnson took an interest in such ideas.

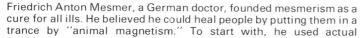

Friedrich Anton Mesmer, a German doctor, founded mesmerism as a cure for all ills. He believed he could heal people by putting them in a trance by "animal magnetism." To start with, he used actual

magnets. Here his patients were placed around a bucket filled with water and iron filings, and told to touch the site of their ailment with a hook placed in the bucket. Mesmer's clinic in Paris was all the rage.

Animals and birds in the news

France, 1713
Jean Charles Hervieux de Chanteloup, canary-keeper to the princess of Condé, has just published his *New Treatise on Canary Birds*. In it he describes several different varieties: yellow, agate, cream, albino, and multicolored.

Spain, 1713
In accordance with the Treaty of Utrecht, which ends the War of the Spanish Succession, the soldiers of the British army have taken possession of the Rock of Gibraltar. They have found it to be inhabited by monkeys! Since there is a ruling that occupying forces must leave the local inhabitants alone, the monkeys will be allowed to remain on the Rock as long as English troops continue to be stationed there. It is said at the Spanish court that King Philip V is consoling himself for his defeat with the thought of the tricks that his former "subjects" will certainly play on their new rulers.

Afghanistan, 1722
On their return from Afghanistan, some travelers have reported with amazement that the local princes use dromedaries to pull along their army cannons.

Portugal, 1723
The Jesuit fathers who have been in Abyssinia as missionaries tell us that the inhabitants of the country not only keep rhinoceroses, but also tame and train them for work. The missionaries give the great beasts milk and watermelons daily, and send them out to pasture with their cows.

Saxony, 1729
The Grand Elector Augustus II (who is also King Augustus I of Poland) presented a great animal combat at Dresden on September 6. As well as three ordinary bulls, there was an aurochs, an enormously large wild ox. As its opponent, a fine stallion was sent into the enclosure, but one blow of the powerful aurochs's horns almost killed the horse. (from the *Mercure de France*)

The Duchy of Bar, 1733
In the Contrisson region of Lorraine, a plague of field mice has already caused considerable damage to the harvest and is now threatening to destroy the newly sown crops. The bishop has called for prayers and processions, but so far these have not been effective in getting the vermin to leave. The villages have now lodged a complaint with Etienne Griffon, a police officer, asking him to summons these baleful creatures in order to put a stop to their invasion. Maître Jacques Collinet, assistant to the procurator general of Lorraine, has obtained from the law courts a judgment against the undesirables, "ordering that three days hence the said mice shall withdraw and shall have no food or nourishment other than that obtainable in the woods adjoining and adjacent to the boundaries of Contrisson, that is to say, the river and its boundaries, being an area four feet long, so that in future they shall be rendered incapable of harming or endangering the produce of the soil of whatever nature this may be."

This, in short, clearly states that henceforth only the Woods of Dauzelle, La Haie Herbelin, and Faux Miroir will be reserved for the field mice.

Canada, 1735
The "Kings's Road," the first highway to link Quebec and Montreal on the left bank of the Saint Lawrence River, which was opened last year by the architect-in-chief Jean Eustache Lanouiller de Boisclerc, has had to be reconstructed in several places owing to the activities of beavers who have been tunneling beneath it to build their "lodges." This has rendered the highway in danger of collapse.

Picardy, 1735
The judges at the Clermont Law Court have condemned an ass, convicted of biting its new mistress, to be shot.

Italy, 1739

Some new blood was needed for the herd of dromedaries installed in 1662 by the duke of Tuscany, Ferdinand II, on his estates at San Rossoro near Pisa. Twenty animals have just arrived from Tunis, thirteen males and seven females, to complete the herd, which is already over a hundred strong. They sell for at least 40 gold *louis* each.

Their living quarters are similar to their original environment—a flat, sandy area near the mouth of the river Arno, covered with shrubs and brambles.

From the age of four the young dromedaries are trained to carry loads. Their hair is used for stuffing mattresses and weaving coarse material. Their skins are put to use, too. However, the milk and flesh of the animals are not consumed, as is the custom in the East.

Siberia, 1743

A Turkoman mission led by one Sepehr Tokhtoglou has arrived at Tobolsk, charged with the task of obtaining some gyrfalcons and white goshawks for the Emir of Bukhara.

This region of Siberia is particularly noted for the fine quality and great numbers of these hawking birds.

United Provinces, 1747

We hear that in Holland several showmen are traveling from town to town with some sea cows and a rhinoceros. The rhinoceros, now aged eight and a half, was captured in the year 1741 in Asia, in the empire of the Great Mogul in Assam Province. It was then taken to the Low Countries from Bengal by its owner, Captain Douvemont van der Meer. The animal eats 60 pounds of hay and 20 pounds of bread every day and drinks 14 buckets of water.

Professor Albinus of Leyden has had an engraving made of it, and the anatomist Petrus Camper has come from the north of Holland in order to study it and make drawings and models.

France, 1749

The Dutch rhinoceros arrived at Versailles early in the year, having journeyed through Stuttgart and Rheims where the curious were able to admire it in its cage, built on a heavy wagon drawn by 20 horses. The king had to abandon his idea of buying it since Captain van der Meer was asking the colossal price of 100,000 *ecus*. The animal was put on exhibition at the Saint Germain Fair where for 30 *sous* its owner sold to those who wanted it a portrait of the curious beast, together with a short pamphlet written by Monsieur Lavocat, who is the librarian of the

Sorbonne.

The rhinoceros has been an enormous success in this country. The artist Jean Baptiste Oudry has painted its portrait, and it has even had an influence on fashion. Elegant Frenchwomen are sporting "rhinoceros" ribbons, and the young sparks have invented a "rhinoceros harness"!

Thank heavens the animal has now left Paris for Lyons and the Midi. Indeed, it is said to have already arrived in Italy. At one time there was a rumor

that it had perished in a shipwreck at sea, together with its owner and all the money it has earned for him—but this was merely a false report spread about to arouse the curiosity of the public.

Italy, 1751

It cannot be denied that the traveling rhinoceros is still drawing large numbers of sightseers. This year it was one of the attractions during the festivities of the Venice Carnival, where all the merrymakers thronged to see and admire it. Since then it has been on show in the amphitheater at Verona, where a medal of its likeness was struck.

England, 1754

King George II has decided to allow the public to view the very fine and well stocked menagerie which he has installed in the Tower of London. However, visitors must either pay an entrance fee of 3 halfpence a head or contribute a cat or a dog to feed to the lions.

These large and ferocious animals are kept in semicircular cages. They include several lionesses who live there with their cubs.

Bavaria, 1755

The margrave of Ansbach has drawn up a list of the game he has caught hunting with his trained falcons over the last 25 years. The total is 1,763 kites; 4,147 herons; 4,857 crows; 1,674 magpies; 14,087 partridges; 985 pheasants; 398 wild ducks; and 5,059 hares.

France, 1757

C.M. Geoffroy has recently published a work entitled *Further Treatise on Medicine*. The author has devoted a whole chapter to the benefits of castoreum, a substance extracted from the glands of the beaver, which can be used as an ingredient in purgatives. "Mixed with purgatives it can be used to hasten their functioning, expressly stimulating and cleansing slow moving bowels, for when it is given on its own in a strong dose it acts as a purgative."

Italy, 1760

". . . In Naples there is a group of monks who keep a herd of pigs whose upkeep is paid for by the local people, in addition to the financial support they give to the monastery. These privileged swine are called 'holy pigs' by the pious men of God to whom they belong. They walk unhindered through the streets and enter houses, where they are received with every politeness. If a sow gives birth, she and her piglets are given every attention by the people she has honored as her hosts for the occasion.

Anyone dealing a blow to a *porco sacro* would be guilty of sacrilege. Despite this, one of them was killed by a group of soldiers lacking in such scruples. The murder caused a great outcry, and the town and senate ordered a rigorous investigation. Fearing discovery, the miscreants bought two church candles, lit them, and stood them at each side of the *porco sacro,* over which they laid a large cloth. Then they placed a vessel of holy water with a sprinkler at its head and a crucifix at its feet. All those who came to visit the corpse found them praying on their knees around the departed. One of them presented the sprinkler to the head of police, who sprinkled holy water around, knelt to pray, and then inquired who the dead person was. The soldiers answered, 'It's one of our comrades—what an honest fellow he was! His death is a great loss. But that's how the world goes, the good are taken, the wicked remain!'" *(From a letter by Diderot to Sophie Volland, dated September 25)*

England, 1764

An East India Company vessel has brought back two tigers destined for the duke of Cumberland's hunt. Although this item of news was reported in the most reliable *Gazette de France*, it is likely that the animals in question are not tigers but leopards. Those very swift creatures are often employed in India to hunt the antelope, notably by the rajah of Baroda, who owns some very well trained leopards.

Franche-Comté, 1767

In the region of Besançon, such thick clouds of butterflies recently alighted that the curé of the town believed them to be devils incarnate and decided to exorcise them. Armed with the ritual robes and instruments of exorcism, he advanced towards the insects. However, they suddenly gathered in such masses that they blocked out the light from the sky. The holy man could not see to read out the awesome words which should have routed these satanic creatures.

India, 1770

Monsieur Chevalier, governor of French India, has sent King Louis XV a two-year-old elephant. Setting off from Chandernagore, it made the entire journey on foot, apart from the crossing of the Bosporus. Last December 27, under the safeguard of Messieurs Lagagneur and Trevisang, the animal arrived in Paris, where an engraving has been made of its likeness after a drawing by Louis Joseph Watteau. At the foot of the print is inscribed the following verse: "Without a pang I leave the Asian strand,
And never shall regret my native land,
Content to live forever and a day
Beneath a much-loved monarch's mighty sway."

Lorraine, 1773

Madame d'Armentières, wife of the governor of Metz, has persuaded her husband to reprieve the thirteen cats that were due to be burned at the stake next June 23. This custom started in 1344 when there was a terrible epidemic of Saint Vitus' dance. It was thought to be the work of satan, who appeared in the form of a black cat. To keep him at bay, thirteen cats have been burned on Saint John's Eve every year. The two highest ranking town officials, the governor and the municipal magistrate, had the honor of heading a procession and setting light to the faggots while the crowd danced around.

France, 1774

Léonard, hairdresser to the queen of France, has created a new hairstyle called "The Cloud of Sentiments," in the tracery are mingled various exotic objects, including some parrots. The duchess of Chartres is now wearing one of these wigs. Its contents include one of her own pet parrots, which she has had stuffed and fixed on a branch.

Bibl. Nat. Paris

Sweden, 1775

The menagerie at Stockholm is at present displaying an extremely curious animal that could be taken for a cross between a horse and a zebra. It is in fact a quagga, a native of southern Africa, which was described for the first time in 1756. This equine creature is striped only around the head, the neck, and the shoulders. It is said that the Dutch colonists who founded Capetown in 1652 killed a great number of them, and used their skins to make leather for grain sacks.

France, 1775

At the Fair of Saint Germain this year, there were, as always, a large number of white cockatoos. This year they were a particularly prominent feature of the fair.

Russia, 1775

Mr. Suderland, the banker, who has chosen to live at the court of Catherine II, has had a very unfortunate misadventure. Wishing to attract the attention of his sovereign, he presented her with a charming little pug-dog, which the empress named after him. Alas, the little dog died, and in order to keep his memory alive the czarina decided "to have Suderland stuffed." Naturally the palace steward was somewhat surprised to receive such a horrible order, but dared not say a word about it. He went to see the banker and acquainted him with the terrible news. Poor Mr. Suderland, terrified, ran and threw himself on his knees before his sovereign to beg for mercy! The empress laughed until she cried, and told everyone about the unfortunate Mr. Suderland's misapprehension. Since then, he has completely lost countenance with the courtiers, who make fun of him wherever he goes.

France, 1777

The duke of Croy, the naturalist Monsieur de Buffon, and the Dutch anatomist Petrus Camper have been to the menagerie at Versailles to see the two-horned rhinoceros brought from the Cape in 1770 by Monsieur Bertin, minister of state. Apparently the animal has such sensitive skin that, since its tail is too short to brush away the stinging flies that irritate it, it spends most of its time up to its neck and ears in the soothing water of a tank which had been specially built for it.

Sweden, 1778

The death is reported of Carolus Linnaeus (Carl von Linné), the great and renowned Swedish naturalist. His book, *Species Plantarum*, achieved the concise method of naming plants and animals by genus and species.

Senegal, 1780

The chevalier de Boufflers, governor of Senegal, has presented Queen Marie Antoinette with a gray parrot native to the colony. He has also brought back several types of exotic birds, all of which will go to the large aviaries kept at Saint Ouen by the duke of Nivernais.

France, 1781

On April 16 King Louis XVI gave permission for a bullbaiting to be held in public in Paris, on the Pantin Road outside the Saint Martin Gate. Such a spectacle can only appeal to the blood-thirsty. Several ladies of quality—whom it is best not to name—mingled with the coarse crowd to watch the gory sight of bulls being torn apart by dogs specially trained for this unpleasant purpose.

Afghanistan, 1781

Some travelers report that in the Kabul region of this country they have seen cranes being hunted in a very strange

fashion. First, the hunters bury some children in the sand dunes with only their noses, their mouths, and the palms of their right hands visible. When the birds alight on the sand, the hunters drive them gently toward the children. The cranes approach the buried children, suspecting nothing, and are seized when they get close enough to the children.

France, 1782

On the night of September 24, the elephant acquired by the king in 1770 burst its chains and broke down the doors of the cage in which it has been kept for the past twelve years. While rampaging through the gardens of Versailles, the animal fell in a pond filled with such filthy mire that although he was rescued next morning from his unpleasant plight, he died a few days later. His body, which weighed 500 pounds, was dissected at the Royal Menagerie.

Brittany, 1782

In the diocese of Nantes, the curé of Clisson has exorcised the evil spirits from all the cows of the region by hanging bags of salt around their necks and sprinkling the animals with holy water. This procedure was undertaken in order to ward off the mysterious evil which was causing them to have severe fits of coughing.

France, 1783

There has recently been a stir at Versailles caused by the adventures of two paper manufacturers from the Annonay region. King Louis XVI commanded these inventors of what is said to be a kind of flying machine to give him a demonstration of its performance. Under the circumstances, Joseph and Etienne Montgolfier, who had built a large, richly decorated balloon, decided to test at the same time whether animals could survive a flight in the upper atmosphere. Accordingly, they put a sheep, a cock, and a duck into a large tub attached to the base of the balloon. This amazing experiment took place on September 19. The balloon rose into the air, remained there for eight minutes, and then descended without being damaged in any way. The animals showed no sign of discomfort whatsoever, and it is already being said that the two inventors will now embark on the construction of a "montgolfière", a balloon capable of conveying humans.

This same year there has been serious concern about the health of the noted naturalist, Monsieur de Buffon, who was run over by a carriage in Paris and dragged some way along the street. Monsieur de Buffon, who is 76 years old, bled for 12 hours and shortly afterwards had an acute attack of the gravel. However, he very quickly recovered and retains a finely optimistic spirit. It is true that the members of this great naturalist's family are known for living a long time.

France, 1784

At the Saint Laurent Fair in Paris spectators were fortunate enough to be able to see some seals disporting themselves freely in a large pool of salt water.

United Provinces, 1784

The East India Company has sent to the governor two eighteen-month-old elephants, captured on the island of Ceylon. The animals have been housed near La Haye in Petit Loo House. They have been given the names of Hans and Parkie and enjoy a great deal of freedom, walking wherever they wish in the gardens. The huge beasts have been put in the care of an English keeper named Thomson, a man who knows all there is to know about the care and training of animals.

Hist. Nat. Paris

THE WILD BEAST OF GÉVAUDAN

How a monster wolf was tracked down

Wolves still roamed many parts of Europe, and in France, Germany, and Scandinavia people still believed in werewolves—people who turned into wolves at night and ate human flesh.

Between 1764 and 1767 the province of Gévaudan in France was terrorized by an enormous animal known as "The Wild Beast of Gévaudan." It made its first appearance in the spring of 1764 when it devoured a young shepherdess, Jeanne Boulet, as she guarded her flock. In the next three years, over a hundred men, women, and children met a similar fate, and even stagecoaches came under attack.

In December 1764, The London Magazine *reported that a detachment of dragoons had been sent after the beast, and that the province had offered 1000 crowns to anyone who could kill it. Twice it was thought to have been destroyed. The first time was in May 1765, when a local squire, Monsieur Marlet, and his brothers fired on an enormous creature, "larger than a year-old bullock." But on the evening of that same day a shepherd was set upon a league farther south, and people realized that there must be another beast in the region. On September 21 of that year an unusually large wolf was killed in some woods by Monsieur Antoine de Beauterne, of the king's household, and people breathed freely again. Alas, on December 2, a pair of young cowherds were killed.*

The Gazette de France *published regular reports about the beast's activities, and rumors abounded as to what kind of creature it was. It was said to have huge teeth, an immense tail, reddish fur, and a very unpleasant smell. Was it the devil? A werewolf? Or the work of some wicked person? People recalled the case of the Marjevols family—in 1762, father, mother, and two sons had been publicly hanged for training wolves to terrify travelers so that they could rob them.*

In June 1767, there were two great gatherings at two chapels in the province where local huntsmen went to have their guns and ammunition blessed. Shortly afterwards, on June 18, the beast reappeared and devoured a baby. Immediately the marquis d'Apcher assembled a hunting party and hounds and at daybreak on June 19, the hunters set off in search of the killer. They beat through the woods all day until they reached the slough of La Sogne d'Anvers. There they posted a man called Jean Chastel. He was quietly occupied reading his prayerbook when suddenly a terrifying animal confronted him. Chastel slowly put down his book; then he raised the gun he had had blessed, loaded it with a blessed bullet, and fired. He hit the creature in the shoulder and it fell dead just as the hounds arrived.

The marquis summoned two surgeons who opened up the creature's body in the presence of a doctor, and in its stomach found the thighbone of a child. A number of anguished parents ran to the scene; among them was a man called Antoine Plantin who formally recognized the creature that had carried off and eaten his eleven-year-old daughter the previous March.

The "beast" was in fact only a wolf—or rather, several wolves, of a particularly large and savage breed, and there were no more attacks after this last one had been shot. But it was a long time before the French forgot the stories of the Beast of Gévaudan.

DOGS AND CATS IN EIGHTEENTH-CENTURY EUROPE

In the 18th century people were not as sentimental about domestic animals as they are today, and sometimes they were extremely cruel to cats, dogs, and other creatures. Dogs were generally kept for their usefulness as sheep dogs, guard dogs, and particularly in England, as hunting dogs. Dalmatians were used both for hunting, and for guarding coach travelers; their long legs, striking appearance, and keen hunting instincts warded off many a highwayman.

In Europe lapdogs—small dogs such as pugs and Maltese dogs—became very popular among fashionable people, and in France the poodle became the rage during the reign of Louis XIV. "Poodle barbers" plied a busy trade along the banks of the Seine, clipping the coats of these dogs in various unnatural designs to please the French aristocracy. The English were not interested in these toylike creatures, preferring to concentrate on perfecting their breeds of hunting dogs.

Dogs were also trained to bait bears, bulls, rats, and sometimes lions and stags, and to fight each other to provide public amusement. The British bulldog developed from a breed of terrier whose flat nose and undershot jaw enabled it to hang on to the nose of an enraged bull.

During the century, however, some people began to realize just how cruel these sports were. In England several famous writers protested against such behavior. Sir Richard Steele asked in his famous newspaper, *The Tatler*, what excuse men had "for the death of so many innocent cocks, bulls, dogs, and bears only to make us sport." As early as 1723 a group of humanitarians got together to protest about sports involving animals. However, bullbaiting was not legally abolished until the next century, in 1823.

Cats often came in for a hard time, too. For centuries there had been many superstitions about them, and they were still associated with devil worship and witchcraft. Christian Europe still maintained the pagan tradition of burning cats alive on the Eve of Saint John (Midsummer Eve). At Aix-en-Provence, until 1757, a fine tomcat would be dressed as the infant Jesus, worshipped at a shrine—and finally thrown in a basket onto a huge bonfire in the city square. Witch-hunts were still common, and in country districts many a poor old woman was hunted as a witch simply because she kept a pet cat. John Gay, author of *The Beggars' Opera*, wrote a poem called "The Old Woman and Her Cats" which poured scorn on these out-of-date beliefs.

In towns, people were more realistic. Cats were needed to hunt down rats—and many people realized their value as pets and companions. The painters Gainsborough and

Reynolds were famous cat lovers and the poet Christopher Smart wrote a poem to "My Cat Jeoffrey." A celebrated cat lover was Dr. Johnson, who was sure that cats had feelings and so was careful not to offend them. He used to go out himself to buy oysters for his cat Hodge, "lest the servants, having that trouble, should take a dislike to the poor creature."

Glossary

Agriculture Farming

Alchemy A combination of chemistry and magic that was practiced in the Middle Ages

Archaeology The study of the people, customs, and life of ancient times

Architecture The science or art of building

Aristocracy Any class that is considered superior because of birth, culture, or wealth

Astronomy The science of the sun, moon, planets, and stars

Automaton A machine or mechanical contrivance sometimes designed to resemble a person or animal; a robot

Boyard A member of the high-ranking Russian aristocracy

Bull baiting The once popular sport of setting dogs to attack a tethered bull

Canal A waterway that has been dug through land to provide a means of transportation

Cavalry Soldiers who fight on horses

Censorship The act of examining, then changing or prohibiting books, plays, or news reports in a way that is acceptable to the government or other organization

Charlatan A person who pretends to be more skilled or knowledgeable than he or she really is

Despot A monarch who has unlimited power

Factory A building where things are manufactured

Famine A lack of food in an area; a time of starvation

Festival A day or time of celebrating and feasting, often to commemorate a great event

Freemason A member of a world wide secret society whose aims are mutual aid and friendship

Imperialism The policy of extending the authority of one country over other countries and colonies

Industrial Revolution The change to an industrial society from an agricultural one and to factory production from home manufacturing

Industry Any kind of business, trade, or manufacturing

Infantry Soldiers who have been trained, equipped, and organized to fight on foot

Justice The administration of law

Landed gentry People, usually of aristocratic birth or wealth, or both, who own large estates

Nobility Those who by birth, title, or rank form the highest social class of a country

Parliament The highest lawmaking body of certain countries

Peasant A farmer in the working class

Philosopher A person who tries to find the truth and studies the principles behind all knowledge

Plague A rapidly spreading disease that is very dangerous and causes many deaths

Poverty The state of lacking money or possessions

Puddling A process used to convert pig iron into wrought iron

Quarantined To be isolated from others for a set amount of time to prevent an infectious disease from spreading

Serf A slave who belonged to the land he worked on and was bought and sold with the land

Smallpox A disease with a fever and blisterlike sores that is very contagious

Snuff A powdery tobacco that is inhaled through the nose

Superstition A belief that is unfounded or irrational

Taxation The system or the act of people paying money to support their government

Trade The buying and selling of goods

Vaccination The process of inoculating a person with bacteria of a certain disease to prevent that person from coming down with that disease

Witch A woman who is said to have magical powers and be under the influence of spirits

Workhouse A place where very poor people are lodged and given work

INDEX

1 2 3 4 5 6 7 8–U-88 87 86 85 84 83